Jesus and Mary

HENRI J. M. NOUWEN

Jesus & Mary

Finding Our Sacred Center

ST. ANTHONY MESSENGER PRESS

CINCINNATI, OHIO

Nihil Obstat: Rev. Arthur J. Espelage, O.F.M.
Rev. Edward J. Gratsch

Imprimi Potest: Rev. John Bok, O.F.M.
Provincial

Imprimatur: +R. Daniel Conlon
Archdiocese of Cincinnati
January 19, 1993

Scripture citations are taken from *The New
American Bible With Revised New Testament*,
copyright ©1986 by the Confraternity of
Christian Doctrine, and are used by
permission. All rights reserved.

Cover and book design by Julie Lonneman
Illustrations by A. Brian Zampier, S.M.

ISBN 0-86716-189-2

©1993, Henri J. M. Nouwen
All rights reserved.

Published by St. Anthony Messenger Press
Printed in the U.S.A.

Contents

Foreword

T his book has two parts. The first is a homily given on May 31, 1988, during the Marian Year at St. Michael's Cathedral, Toronto. Henri Nouwen says the inspiration for the homily came during the Holy Week he spent with the Trappists in Holland, Manitoba. Although originally addressed to priests, his words will have meaning and application for all who by Baptism share in the priesthood of Christ.

G. Emmett Cardinal Carter called the homily a "moving and penetrating analysis of the attitude of the Christian toward Mary and the importance of Mary in our spiritual lives. I do not believe that anyone can read these words without being deeply affected."

The second part of the book is Henri Nouwen's journal of his pilgrimage to Lourdes, France, in January 1990, the beginning of a new decade and of a new Europe after the destruction of the Berlin Wall.

Why put these two writings together? Is publishing them in book form just a publisher's ploy?

The compelling reason for publication is that the material is significant. Henri Nouwen, as always, addresses issues that deeply concern his contemporaries. He has been an inspiring spiritual guide for me since I read *Intimacy* (1969) and *The Wounded Healer* (1972). In reading about his journey, we recognize our spiritual journey. Each of his more than thirty books recounts new steps and new insights into the complex, messy, anguishing, exhilarating and redeemed world which we recognize as our own. This homily and journal are important parts of his journey and deserve publication in book form.

Even though they are different genres, there is a twofold unity. First, obviously they are both by Henri Nouwen and about Henri Nouwen. He shares himself. The homily flows from his experience. His trip to Lourdes is not a travelogue but a journal of a prayerful encounter with Jesus and Mary.

In his homily in Toronto Henri Nouwen said that speaking about Mary requires great honesty as well as *simplicity*. He speaks honestly about fears, resentments, jealousies, guilt and shame. We are invited to find our inner child and also to rid ourselves of the "false adulthood" of our times. He defines anguish as "interrupted love" and addresses an "anguishing generation."

"When the love we most need to receive is being withdrawn from us and the love we most want to give is not welcome, then our hearts are torn to pieces and thrown into the darkness of anguish."

But forgiveness and healing, hope, joy, freedom, simplicity and innocence break through. "I too carry God's innocence in me," Henri Nouwen writes. "Before I am sinful, I am innocent; that is, before I participate in the evil of the world, I am touched with goodness.... I have to claim that innocence in me. It belongs to my deepest self."

At Lourdes Henri Nouwen discovers anew "my sacred center." He leaves the shrine of Mary feeling "less tense," "less worried." He urges his listeners in Toronto to trust that the darkness which comes into their lives is "simply a tunnel and not a final destination."

Not only does he speak honestly but he speaks simply. He has studied psychology at the Catholic University of Nijmegen and spent two years as a fellow in the program for psychiatry and religion at the Menninger Foundation. He has taught at Amsterdam's Pastoral Institute, the universities of Notre Dame, Yale and Harvard. He has lived with the Trappists at Genesee, the poor in Latin America and mentally handicapped adults in l'Arche communities in Toronto and France. But he does not quote from books. His words come simply from his experience and his heart.

The second basis of unity is that both parts of the book deal with Henri Nouwen's insights into his relationship with Jesus and Mary. He experiences Mary as his "gentle guide" who takes him by the hand and leads him into deeper union with her son. She can lead "beyond debates and discussions in our Church, beyond the complexities of contemporary psychology and sociology, beyond all the wounds and hurts of your own heart, and brings you to that place in your innermost self where Jesus dwells."

Mary asks all of us, Henri Nouwen says, to let our hearts become more and more childlike, and she "creates a space for us where we can become children...." The mother of the suffering Jesus asks more—that "we let our hearts be broken by the anguish of our world."

"Mary calls me back to where I most want to be: to the heart of God which...is also the heart of the world."

Intimacy with Jesus, Henri Nouwen says, simplifies his life. His resolve is that the risen Jesus "become ever more the center of my life...

the heart of my heart, the fire of my life, the lover of my soul, the bridegroom of my spirit."

"All that there is of love in me is a gift of Jesus, yet every gesture of love I am able to make is uniquely mine.... The deeper my intimacy with Jesus, the more complete is my freedom."

It is a privilege to be able to join this extraordinary spiritual guide in his encounter with Jesus and Mary.

Jeremy Harrington, O.F.M.

Mary, Our Mother

Speaking about Mary, the mother of God and now our mother, requires great honesty as well as simplicity. In all honesty, I want to tell you that only recently has Mary come close to me. During this past Holy Week while staying with the Trappists in Holland, Manitoba, I knew that I was being asked to live the death and rising of Jesus in my own flesh, but I also knew that I couldn't do it alone. It would destroy me.

On the day before I left to go to the Trappists, a friend had given me a rosary of the seven sorrows of Mary. Frankly speaking, I didn't even know which the seven sorrows were! But as I learned about them, I realized that this rosary had been given to me so that Mary could show me how to be truly faithful to her Son. "Stabat Mater," Mary stood by me as I asked Jesus to let me die with him and rise with him. She stood by me as I tried to let go of the many people and things that so far had prevented me from being nothing but a child of God. She stood by me as I tried to strip myself of all the busyness, craziness and activism that had made me into a "respected priest." She stood by me as I begged God to raise me up with Jesus into a new life, maybe hidden from the world but visible to God. She stood by me when I expressed, against all the yearnings of my flesh, the desire to know no one but the crucified and risen Lord and to give all of my being into his service.

I tell you honestly that I have never felt so much peace and so much anguish at the same time: the peace that comes from the intimate communion with God's inexhaustible love, the anguish that comes from the rejection of that divine love by a world that pervades also my own flesh.

As I returned from that Holy Week experience, I realized that the invitation to speak to you about Mary was an invitation to speak to you from this experience and to call you with great love, but also great urgency, to live your lives in an ever-greater closeness to Mary. So I am here, not simply to call you to a deeper devotion to Mary but to urge you to enter fully into the School of Mary and let her teach you how to become a living reminder of Jesus, the Prince of Peace, in the midst of an anguished world.

I also want to speak in great simplicity. This is a moment to speak from heart to heart about her who so wants us to remain faithful in the ministry of her son Jesus. As my own heart gradually becomes open to Mary's guidance, I want to let it find connections with your heart so that we become increasingly united in our desire to bring the fire of Jesus' love to the world and make it blaze (see Luke 12:49).

I invite you to look with me first of all at Mary as the mother of the child Jesus, the mother who asks of us that we let our hearts become more and more childlike. Then I want you to look with me at Mary as the mother of the suffering Jesus, the mother who asks of us that we let our hearts be broken by the anguish of our world.

Mary, Mother of the Child Jesus

Mary creates a space for us where we can become children as Jesus became a child. She wants us to live in the world with the deep knowledge of "love the Father has bestowed on us that we may be called the children of God. Yet so we are" (1 John 3:1).

How much I want to say to you, as Jesus said: "Become like children" (see Matthew 18:3). Many of us have become so serious and intense, so filled with preoccupations about the future of the world and the Church, so burdened by our own loneliness and isolation, that our hearts are veiled by a dark sadness, preventing us from exuding the peace and the joy of God's children. You know as well as I that when our words are full of warnings, our eyes full of fears, our bodies full of unfulfilled needs

and our actions full of distrust, we cannot
expect ever to create around us a community
that shines as a light in the darkness.

When Jesus said to his beloved disciple:
"Behold, your mother" (John 19:27), he gave
Mary to us. He wants us to have a mother who

can guide us toward our true childhood, not the childhood of an infant that does not yet know its own wounds, but the childhood of the disciple who has come to see that, underneath all his personal woundedness, there is a first love untainted by the ambiguities and ambivalences of human affection. We need Mary to find our way to the joy and peace of the children of God.

We are constantly being pulled back into the false adulthood of our age. Many of us who want to offer consolation experience deep inner desolation. Many of us who want to offer healing and affection to others experience a seemingly inexhaustible hunger for intimacy. Many of us who are priests speak to others about the beauty of family life, friendship and community, then come home at night to a place that seems more like an empty cave than a true home. Many of us who let water flow on the heads of those who search for a new family, give bread to those who search for a new community, and touch with oil those who search for healing, find ourselves with dry, hungry and sick hearts, restless during the day and anxious during the night. Yes, indeed, many of us have lost touch with our identity as children of God.

But it is precisely this childhood that Mary wants us to claim. She who offered an immaculate space for God to take on human flesh wants to offer us also a space where we can be reborn as Jesus was born. With the same heart that loved Jesus, she wants to love us. It is a heart that will not make us wonder anxiously whether we are truly loved. It is a heart that has not been marked by the infidelities of the human race and so will never bring wounds to those who seek peace there. Jesus has given her to us so that she can guide us as we try to shake off our sadness and open the way to true inner peace.

When we allow Mary to become our mother, she will let us see in a new way that we belong to God who is our Father, our Brother and our Spouse, and so holds us safe in the divine love. Once Mary has taken us beyond the burdens of our human cravings for satisfaction to God's first unconditional love, we will see that love shine through every person we meet on our way. Because once we have experienced God's first love in our own heart, we will be able to see it in the hearts of those to whom we are called to minister. Heart speaks to heart. Spirit speaks to Spirit. God speaks to God. That is the mystery of which we have been made part.

You and I are broken people. We are wounded and we wound others, even when we try to avoid it at all cost. I urge you to look at Mary, the mother of the child Jesus, and let her lead you beyond all the debates and discussions in our Church, beyond all the complexities of contemporary psychology and sociology, beyond all the wounds and hurts of your own heart, and bring you to that place in your innermost self where Jesus dwells. Let her speak to you about the desire of Jesus to have you as his disciple, to show you his unique love and to see you full of his peace. Mary says: "Stop arguing, stop fighting, stop doubting, stop hesitating. Come with me deeper and deeper into the center of your own being. There you will find how much you are loved. There you will find who you truly are: the favored child of God, the brother or sister of Jesus, the temple of the Holy Spirit."

When you have allowed Mary to guide you to a new childhood, then you will be free to move into the world and suffer there in Jesus' name.

Mary, the Mother of the Suffering Jesus

She who embraced Jesus as a vulnerable child also embraced him as the man who had fulfilled his mission through suffering.

The death of Jesus plunged Mary into the most intense anguish that has ever been lived by a human being, except for Jesus himself. She is truly the compassionate mother. Her heart is pierced by the suffering and death of her Son in and through whom all human anguish is lived. The purity that made Mary the mother of the child Jesus also made her the mother of the man of sorrows. She who could not wound her Son was most sensitive to his wounds. Therefore, she whose peace was deepest also lived in the deepest anguish. Her anguish and the anguish of Jesus are as intimately connected as her peace was connected with the peace of Jesus. Peace and anguish are both part of her motherhood. When the wounded body of Jesus is laid in her arms, Mary holds the anguish of the whole world, suffered by Jesus. Thus, she becomes the mother of all whose anguish Jesus has lived and died for.

Sisters and brothers, look at Mary as she holds the broken body of her son. There we can see our vocation to open our own arms to those who suffer and to let them discover that, in communion with Jesus, they can live their anguish without losing their peace. You know, but constantly forget, just as I do, that our vocation is not to take away human suffering but to reveal that through Jesus the suffering has become the way to the glory of God.

In our production-minded world we are tempted to ask ourselves what our unique contribution is in comparison with the contributions of doctors, lawyers, social workers, psychologists and psychotherapists. Such comparisons often lead us to a very low self-esteem and make us wonder whether we have anything at all to offer. But as witnesses of Jesus we should resist radically such comparisons and realize that—as Jesus himself—we are not sent into the world to take away human anguish but to share it and thus proclaim in our own bodies the ultimate victory of love. And, in fact, we do share it every time we do not run away from the anguish of God's people but receive it in faith.

There is so much anguish. You know it not only from observation of other people's suffering, but also from the reflection on your own most intimate pain. You know about the ruptures in families, friendships and communities; you know about the desperate search for intimacy, fellowship, home or anything that can offer a sense of belonging. You know that, as the world gets more sophisticated, more scientific, more technical and, therefore, more complex, distant and unfamiliar, human anguish increases. Teenagers commit suicide, young couples can't stay together, sexual relationships become violent, children become strangers to their parents, adult men and women no longer experience work as an expression of mature life, many pastoral ministers lose heart and dissipate their energies, old people feel cut off from their families and the dying often wonder if they should ask for intervention to shorten their pain.

You know it so well because you yourself are part of this anguishing generation. Anguish is interrupted love. When the love we most need to receive is being withdrawn from us and the love we most want to give is not welcome, then our hearts are torn to pieces and thrown into the darkness of anguish. Jesus suffered this anguish with us and for us unto death. Mary received the dead body of Jesus and her heart, too, was pierced by sorrow.

I know now that to be truly faithful to my vocation, I must go to Mary. Jesus has given her to me so that I can be a truly compassionate priest, a priest who wants to receive the body of Christ and thus live in sorrow with the suffering world. But is it possible to live such a compassionate life in our success- and efficiency-oriented society? Mary says: "Have courage, I am holding you close to Jesus. Yes, you are called to carry the burden and the yoke of my Son, which is the burden and yoke of the whole suffering world. But do not be anxious for his burden is light and his yoke is easy. Go to him for he is gentle and humble of heart and there with him you will find rest for your souls."

I am discovering in my own life as a priest that without Mary I cannot fully enter into the mystery of Jesus' compassionate love. It is hard to explain why this is so, but I see now, mostly retrospectively, how I used to speak more *about* Jesus than *to* him. Most of all, I see now how Jesus had become more an argument for the moral life than the door to the mystical life which is the life in communion with God, Father, Son and Holy Spirit. Mary calls me back to where I most want to be: to the heart of God which, as you know, is also the heart of the world. She calls me to let the passion of Jesus become my passion and his glory become my glory. She calls me to move beyond the dos and don'ts of the morally correct life into an intimacy with God where I can live the sadness, pain and anguish of this world while already tasting the gladness, joy and peace of the glorified Lord.

Mary didn't just call *me* to that life. She also invites *you* to that same life. That is why with great urgency I ask you to go to Mary and learn from her how to live in this anguishing world as peace-bringing witnesses of her Son.

Conclusion

Mary is the mother of the child Jesus. Mary, too, is the mother of the suffering Jesus. While dying on the cross, Jesus gave his mother to us so that she could show us the way to a new childhood, as well as the way to enter into deep solidarity with the anguished, suffering world.

Every time a priest takes the bread and the cup with wine and says, "This is my body, this is my blood," he offers God's people the spiritual food and drink that makes them brothers and sisters of Jesus and participants in his anguish. The Eucharist is the mystery that lets both the peace and the anguish of Jesus shape our hearts and so deepen our faith, strengthen our hope and purify our love.

"Stabat Mater," Mary stood there. She did

not succumb in her sorrow. She stood in her
sorrow deeply rooted in the peace of Jesus. She
still stands under the cross of our suffering
humanity. Each time we lift up the bread of life

and the cup of salvation and thus connect the
very concrete daily pain of people with the one,
all-embracing sacrifice of Jesus, Mary is there
and says: "Become what you are, a true
disciple of Jesus, taken, blessed, broken and
given."

Dear sisters and brothers, let us put all our

trust in her. She will teach us at every moment of our lives how to choose the narrow road and so become more and more disciples with a heart broken for the world, but a heart from which comes both water and blood.

Lourdes: At the Beginning of a New Decade

Introduction: Not Berlin, But Lourdes

Today is January 7, 1990, and I am in Lourdes. A few weeks ago I felt convinced I should go to Berlin to experience the radical changes taking place in Europe at the beginning of a new decade. I didn't go. I am not completely sure why not, but when I gave careful attention to my inner voice, I knew that I had to stay away from large crowds, noisy debates and great political movements. The next decade is one that will change radically the face of our planet. The question for me was: How to live that decade?

The answer came quickly: in deep communion with Jesus. Jesus has to be and to become ever more the center of my life. It is not enough that Jesus is my teacher, my guide, my source of inspiration. It is not even enough that he is my companion on the journey, my friend and my brother. Jesus must become the heart of my heart, the fire of my life, the lover of my soul, the bridegroom of my spirit. He must become my only thought, my only concern, my only desire. The thousands of people, events, ideas and plans that occupy my inner life must become all one in the one and only name: Jesus.

I know that I have to move from speaking about Jesus to letting him speak within me, from thinking about Jesus to letting him think within me, from acting for and with Jesus to letting him act through me. I know the only way for me to see the world is to see it through his eyes. Everything has to become very simple, very unified, very focused. It is no longer a question of being up to date or well-informed. At this moment in history—my own as well as that of the world—I have to go to the very center of being: the center where time touches eternity, where earth and heaven meet, where God's Word becomes human flesh, where death and immortality embrace. There is really no longer a question of options. With an unmistakable clarity I have heard a voice saying, "Give me everything, and I will give you everything."

And so, I didn't go to Berlin. Instead I went, from my temporary base at l'Arche in Trosly to Compiègne, from Compiègne to Paris and from there to Lourdes.

There are very few pilgrims at this time of the year. I am here alone. After the long, tiring night on the train, I arrived at "the little convent" of the Sisters of the Immaculate Conception at 7:30 a.m. I slept, went to the grotto where Mary appeared to Bernadette, celebrated the Eucharist of the Epiphany in the basilica and prayed.

Why am I here? To give my life to Jesus. To make Jesus the very center of my existence. But how is this to come about? Mary is here to show me, Mary is here to be my gentle counselor, to take me by the hand and let me enter into full communion with her son.

I am afraid, but Mary is here and tells me to trust. I realize that I can make Jesus the heart of my heart only when I ask Mary to show me how. She is the mother of Jesus. In her, God interrupted history and started to

make everything new. And so I too have to put myself under her protection as I seek to enter the 90's with Jesus alone.

As I live these days, I want to stay away from all the big news on TV and radio. For just a while, I want to fast from political, economic and religious debates. I simply want to be very close to her who spoke to Bernadette in the grotto. I trust that she will open my heart for a new encounter with Jesus.

The Water: A Call to Purity

Today is the feast of the Baptism of Jesus, a dark and rainy day. At the grotto, everything speaks of water: the rushing Gave River, the drizzling rain from the cloudy sky, the spring of Masabielle. There are few pilgrims. The large space before the grotto is empty. Here

and there I see people with their umbrellas
walking close to the place where Mary spoke to
Bernadette. They touch the rocks forming the
cave, watch the little spring, let their rosaries
move through their fingers, look up to the
statue of Mary, make the sign of the cross and
light a candle. It is gray, cold, damp and
empty. No music, no songs, no processions.

I want to be purified. I want to be cleansed.
I go to the baths. There, two men instruct me to
undress. They wrap a blue apron around my
waist, ask me to concentrate on what
intercessions I want to ask of Mary, then lead
me into the bath and immerse me in the ice-
cold water. When I stand again, they pray the
Hail Mary with me and give me a cup of water
from the spring to drink. There are no towels
with which to dry myself. And so, still
shivering and wet, I put my clothes back on, go

back to the grotto and pray. Looking up at the statue, I read the words: "I am the Immaculate Conception," and I understand. The people of Israel were led through the Red Sea; Jesus was baptized in the Jordan; someone poured water over my head shortly after I was born. Blessed are the pure of heart; they shall see God.

I am looking. I am listening. Do I see and hear? I want to, but I cannot force myself. Bernadette saw a young woman dressed in white and blue. She saw her smile, she heard her voice. On this dark, rainy day there is little to please the senses: no sun, no foliage, no candlelight. Under little tin-roofed stalls, some men are burning candles in bunches of hundreds, but it doesn't warm my heart. Everything comes back to the basic questions: "Do you want to see? Do you want to let go of your sin? Do you want to repent?" I do, I do, but

I do not know how to make it happen.

I walk from the grotto to the basilica above it. Many steps lead me to the little square overlooking the valley of the Gave. Entering the crypt of the church where the Blessed Sacrament is adored during the day, I see the host enclosed in a large glass triangle held up by a tree-like structure. A few people are praying. It is very quiet. I sit down before the altar on which the Blessed Sacrament rests.

After an hour, I sense a deep need for forgiveness and healing. I go to a priest in the chapel of confessions across the way from the basilica. He speaks to me for a long time. His French is difficult for me to understand. I strain to listen. He mentions the poverty of Lourdes in January and says, "It is good for you to be here now. Pray to Mary and Bernadette and be willing to let go of the old and let God's grace touch you as it touched Mary and Bernadette. Don't be afraid to be poor, alone, naked, stripped of all your familiar ways of doing things. God is not finished with you yet." I listen and I know he speaks in Jesus' name. He absolves me of all my sins and tells me to say a prayer that reminds me that I belong to God. I shake hands with this stranger-friend and I feel a little lighter.

Evening is approaching. I walk along the promenade where, during the summer, thousands of people—young and old, sick and healthy—pray and sing. No one is there now.

Leaving the grounds of the grotto, I enter a coffee shop attached to a souvenir store. I used to hate Lourdes "kitsch": the plastic madonnas and plastic Bernadettes in all sizes and styles. But today I don't have that feeling. I buy two little statues for a handicapped woman who

knew I was coming to Lourdes. She had lost
her phosphorescent madonna and asked me to

buy her a new one. To be sure I buy two. The man who sells them to me is all smiles. I sit down in the coffee shop and order a cappuccino with a pastry. The woman tells me the pastry will taste better when hot. She heats it for me and asks me how I like it. I am the only one in the shop. I stay for an hour reading a book.

At 6 p.m. I pass the grotto again. I pray for a while. A man in a plastic coat is sweeping away the water and arranging the candles. A few people sit in the grotto praying their rosaries. It is very quiet. The floodlight has been turned on to mark the cave, the statue and the altar in the cave.

It is dark and still raining when I leave to go back to "the little convent." I hold my rosary in my hands and say the Hail Mary with a loud voice as I walk home. Only the barren trees along the Gave can hear me. My whole being prays for purity: purity of mind, purity of heart, purity of body. I remember the prayer my mother taught me: "By your Immaculate Conception, O Mary, purify my body and sanctify my soul." I say it again and feel a little bit of peace touching me from within.

The Stone: A Call to Simplicity

The next morning as I leave "the little convent," it is soft outside. Here and there behind the clouds I see a few patches of blue sky. The rain has stopped. Before my leaving for Lourdes, my friend Mirella told me to be sure to make the Stations of the Cross. These are life-size representations of fourteen moments in the Passion of Jesus placed along a small path, beside a winding road leading to the top of a tree-covered hill. To encourage me,

Mirella had given me a little book with reflections on the stations by Thomas Philippe, O.P. With the booklet in my hands I enter the park where the stations are placed. I am alone.

After a few minutes' walk, I arrive at the first station: "Jesus is condemned to death." Looking up, I see a long stairway leading up to a bronze statue of Jesus staring down at me. Around him stand a group of fierce Roman soldiers. A multilingual sign reads: "Please go up the stairs on your knees." I do, even though there are large puddles of water on the steps. As I crawl to the top and come closer to the statue of Jesus facing me, I get a deep sense of being like Peter. The figure of a small boy carrying a bowl and towel reminds me of Pilate's washing his hands in front of the crowds and declaring his innocence. Who is innocent in front of the innocent One? Who does not participate in his condemnation? As I come so close to the statue that I can touch it, I see that many visitors have written their names on Jesus' cloak. What were they trying to express? At one place I read: Joan, Michael, Francine and Ron. What went through the minds of these people when they marked the image of Jesus with their names?

As I walk up the hill, I see Jesus falling three times; I witness his encounters with Mary, Simon of Cyrene, Veronica and the weeping women. I see Jesus robbed of his clothes, nailed to the cross and dying between two criminals. And I stand in front of the Pieta: Mary holding the dead body of Jesus in her lap. Then the road takes me down again to the bottom of the hill. There I spy a great cave and, in front of it, eleven statues circling the body of Jesus before it is laid in the tomb. I stand there for a long time reading Thomas Philippe's reflection about the last station. He writes about the tomb of my life where I must bury my old self. He says:

> The Christian life is a continual struggle against the old self. Not just a struggle in the sense of a battle, but a real putting in the tomb.... All authentic Christian lives...know these long "tunnels" where one does not see anything anymore, where one understands

nothing, where one is disgusted. Jesus makes us descend with him in the tomb, in the weakness, in the darkness, in everything that seems dead in our heart, but always to rectify us, to purify us, to liberate us.

As I look into the long deep dark cave in the rock and see the body of Jesus carried into that darkness, I want to enter with him and let all my selfish needs and desires, all my violence,

resentments, lusts and petty jealousies be put there, never to be taken up again. I pray for hope, for courage and, most of all, for trust that the darkness is simply a tunnel and not a final destination. It seems such an endless struggle, and I often wonder if I will ever see the end of this dark passage.

As I walk away from the last station expecting to find the exit from the park, I turn a corner and suddenly see a huge, round stone. From its center many rays are carved, reaching out to its far edges. It looks like the sun, it speaks of light and freedom. Its simplicity stops me in my tracks. There are no statues, no gestures, no movements. Just a great, round free-standing boulder. Beside it are the words: "At the first sign of dawn...they found that the stone had been rolled away." Turning to the other side of the stone I read:

"He has risen, as he said he would."

An immense solitude and peace come over me. I am quite alone: no people, no statues, no events to think about. Just that huge stone. All the stations of the Passion, so full of drama and tragedy, seem to be gone. All that remains is this very quiet place—empty, simple, pure and unpretentious. I had not expected this "fifteenth station." It's not really a station. It's more like a gentle reminder, a moment of hope, a small rearrangement of nature. It does not demand my attention as did the life-size figures of the stations. I can pass it by and let it go unnoticed. But something is happening within me—a leaping up.

I have often made the stations of the cross, in many places and circumstances, but here I stand, surprised by a joy I didn't expect to come to me at the end of this long walk. It is the utter simplicity of it all that touches me most. The Resurrection of Jesus simplifies everything. Life is so complex. There are so, so many memories, so many events, so many possibilities. There are people to pay attention to, events to reflect on, choices to ponder. And there is the ongoing question of priorities: who to respond to first, what to consider first, where to go first.... But here before the rolled-away stone, a simple center from which hope radiates, all is very simple. I sense the deep truth of this simplicity. Jesus is risen. All has become one. The emptiness of the place makes me realize that I don't have to go anywhere, meet anyone, do anything. All is here, now, in this instant.

Gone are all those emotions felt while crawling up the steps and looking at the condemned Jesus. Gone too are all feelings of

guilt and shame. Gone as well are all the
questions about what to do in the years ahead.

The risen Jesus is not bound to any place or
person. He is totally free. Simplicity and
freedom belong together. Purity too. I realize
that I need not be at Lourdes to find peace and
joy. Lourdes simply reminds me that purity,
simplicity and freedom belong to the heart and
can be lived anywhere.

Mary met Jesus after the Resurrection,
but not as he was met by Mary of Magdala or
John or Peter or the disciples on the road to
Emmaus. She didn't need to be convinced of
anything. Her heart was so simple, so pure, so
free that her encounter with her risen son
could be completely interior. A heart that truly
knows Jesus doesn't need an apparition. Jesus
and Mary were always present to each other in
sorrow and joy. I know now that the purer and

simpler my heart is, the more clearly I will see—wherever I am.

I leave the park. Cars rush by. I walk to the town and buy lunch in the same coffee shop I visited yesterday. The lady is happy to see me again and serves me with special kindness. A young man writes in his notebook while eating his lunch. When I ask him where he is from, he says, "From Brazil." I feel an urge to find out more about him, but something tells me it is better to remain silent, enfold him in my prayer and walk back to the grotto.

The Grotto: A Call to Innocence

After three days in Lourdes, I know it is time to go home. When I came I had thought about staying a week, maybe even two weeks. But as I prayed at the grotto, in the crypt and on the hill of the Stations of the Cross, it became very clear that staying more than three days would not be good. I have received all I could expect to receive. The time for asking has passed. Now I have to live the life I am so clearly called to live: simple, pure, free.

Last night I sat in front of the grotto holding a large candle in my hands. It would take more than a day for the candle to burn down, but I wanted to be, for a while, with the flame that would pray all through the night. I prayed for all the people who surround me close by, as well as for those far away. As I looked at the statue of Mary in the niche above the grotto, I lifted up to her not only all those who are part of my family, my community, my circle of friends, but all the people whose lives will go through so many changes in the coming decade. Ten years from now the world will be so different. How will it look? Will there be peace? Will there be less hunger and starvation, less persecution and torture, less homelessness and AIDS? Will there be more unity, more love, more faith? I have no answers to these questions. I know nothing of the future. I don't have to. But I pray for all the people who will journey with me over the next decade and ask Mary to keep them all close to her son.

A taxi brings me to the railroad station. The driver tells me there are 420 hotels in Lourdes and that every year between Easter and the first of November close to five million pilgrims come to the grotto to pray to Mary. With a smile he says, "You are not in that number, you come out of season."

It takes from 8:30 in the morning until 4:30 in the afternoon to travel from Lourdes to

Paris. As I sit in the train, I let the landscape slip by. My thoughts are of Mary, Bernadette and the ten years ahead of me. The word that comes to mind is "innocent." Mary was innocent. Her soul wasn't wounded by sin. That is why she could offer a perfect place to the child of God. Her innocence was an innocence from which the Word of God could take flesh and become the lamb to take away the sin of the world. Her innocence made her become the Mother of Sorrows because she who had no sin sensed more deeply the sins of humanity for which her son came to suffer and die.

I think of Bernadette. She was only fourteen when she saw the "Lady." Everything I have read and heard about her makes me aware of how simple and clear-headed she was. She would be the last to desire an apparition and, when she saw the Lady at the grotto, she remained quite aloof in the midst of all the confusion that followed. She stated what she saw and heard—no more, no less— and stuck to it no matter what people said of her or did to her. She possessed a true innocence: simple, straightforward, clear-minded, unaffected by the sensational responses in her surroundings. Bernadette wanted nothing for herself, but only to mediate the message of the Lady. She must have been a very strong person, free from the usual manipulations of people. Her innocence was that of a child who knows she is loved and trusts her own sense of what is good and worthy. It was with her innocence that Bernadette could see and hear the mother of Jesus and be a simple, unambiguous witness to her words about prayer and penance.

Lourdes: At the Beginning of a New Decade

The train goes fast. After Bordeaux, it
stops only at Tours before arriving at Paris. I
talk to two women in the dining car. They don't
know each other, but both are connected with
the French diplomatic corps and have traveled
widely: Argentina, Nigeria, Lebanon, the
Emirates, Niger, Germany, Switzerland and
so on. I see a lot of suffering in their faces, but
I see also a simple human goodness underlying
all the disillusionments of an ever-changing
life. I keep thinking of innocence, and I sense
that beyond all my own darkness there is
innocence too. Like Mary and Bernadette and
these two traveling women, I too carry God's
innocence in me. Before I am sinful, I am
innocent; before I participate in the evil of the
world, I am touched with goodness. I realize
after my days in Lourdes that I have to claim
that innocence in me. It belongs to my deepest

self. It is given to me by God my Creator; it is reclaimed for me by Jesus my Redeemer. It is this innocence that makes me hear the voice that says, "You are my son, my beloved; on you my favor rests" (see Luke 3:22).

I know that I am called to live at the place of innocence: the place where Jesus chose to live. There he made his home and asks me to make mine. In that place I am loved and well held. There I do not have to be afraid. And from there I can forgive and heal and make things new.

The countryside between Tours and Paris is peaceful: many green fields, here and there touched by a few rays of sun breaking through the clouds. Can I live innocently on this planet in the years ahead? Can I choose to make my innocence my home, think from there, speak from there, act from there? It is a hard choice because my insecure self wants so much to be part of a world that controls, rewards and tells me whether I am good or bad. But I can go beyond that insecurity and discover my sacred center, fashioned in secret and molded in the depths of the earth.

I know that every time I choose for my innocence I don't have to worry about the next ten years. I can simply be where I am, listening, seeing, touching in the very moment, always sure that I am not alone but with him who called me to live as God's child. Jesus prays to his Father for his disciples, saying: "I do not ask that you take them out of the world but that you keep them from the evil one. They do not belong to the world any more than I belong to the world. Consecrate them in the truth" (John 17:15-17). My innocence is hidden in God. As a child who belongs to God,

I can claim my innocence without leaving the world. In fact, as an innocent one, I am sent into the world: "As you sent me into the world, so I have sent them into the world" (John 17:18).

Within a few minutes I will arrive in Paris, at the Austerlitz station. It is the city of saints and sinners, Jerusalem and Babylon, a constant invitation to prayer and a constant bombardment of the senses. It is the city of Notre Dame and the Place de Pompidou, the city of hidden holiness and spectacular exhibitions. I have to walk through it as the innocent one and trust that I will touch the innocence of my companions in life. I have to trust that whenever I speak from the place of innocence, my words will heal; that whenever I act from the place of innocence, my actions will bring forth life, in Paris or anywhere else.

For the innocent ones there is nothing to fear. They will see God wherever they are. Blessed are the pure of heart. Blessings on Paris. Blessings on the world. Blessings on all of its people.

Conclusion—The Call of the Bridegroom

I am back home again. I find letters on my table and little notes about people who tried to call me. It all looks quite ordinary. A few friends express surprise that I didn't stay longer: "I thought you were going for a week. Why back so soon?" I tell them that I had received all I could hope for and wanted to return to my work. They nod understandingly, but I realize I have a hard time expressing what I feel. As I look out of my window, I see the familiar old chestnut trees and, behind them, the vague contours of the forest of Compiègne. I say to myself, "I must go back to work. But not back to the old way of working." When I left for Lourdes, I felt anxious and tense. My writing wasn't going well. I was trying too hard, pushing too fast, wanting too much. It seemed as though my mind was in cramps. Everything I did was done so deliberately and self-consciously that nothing could flow freely. Every thought, idea, vision or perspective seemed frozen. My inner movements had become spastic. I complained to my friends: "I feel so tense inside—no inspirations, no easy streams of good words, no spontaneity."

Then, suddenly, I left. Not to Berlin to be excited by visions of a new world, but to Lourdes to be alone and let my anxious heart rest. Now, five days later, I am sitting again at my desk. I remember Mother Teresa's words to me twelve years ago: "Write simply," she said, "very simply. People need simple words." I heard that same call again in Lourdes. It is so easy for me to get caught up in complicated thinking. It is hard to be simple because simplicity asks for a pure heart and an innocent eye, qualities which are gifts from God, freely given. I cannot just will them.

Much was given to me at Lourdes. Both Mary and Bernadette brought me close to the pure and innocent heart of Jesus. If there are any words to write, they will come from the Spirit of Jesus in me. I have to let the water of purification cleanse my many old ways of speaking and writing. Many long-standing, "tried and true" patterns must be laid in the tomb. Trusting that the "right" words will be there when they *need* to be there.

I feel less tense now, less anxious, less worried. It was good to be in Lourdes, good to "waste" time just being there among the saints. I have no great new plans, no big new ideas, no vision about the future, I have only the desire to remain close to that place in me where I can hear the voice that calls me, "my son, my beloved," and that will tell me what to do, say or write when the time for it has come. The quiet grotto, the water from the well, the round sun-like stone are signs of hope calling me to remain always open to receive from Jesus the purity, simplicity and innocence I desire. I am not alone. Jesus dwells within me. Whatever is pure, simple and innocent in me comes from him. With his love I can love and give myself to others. With his eyes I can see God's face; with his ears I can hear God's voice; with his heart I can speak to God's heart.

I know that, alone, I cannot see, hear or touch God in the world. But God in me, the living Christ in me, *can* see, hear and touch God in the world, and all that is Christ's in me is fully my own. His simplicity, his purity, his innocence are my very own because they are truly given to me to be claimed as my most personal possessions. That is what Paul means when he says, "I have been crucified with Christ; yet I live, no longer I, but Christ lives in me" (Galatians 2:19, 20). All the beauty of Mary comes from Jesus, yet she is so completely her own. All the sanctity of Bernadette is given to her by Jesus, yet she owns every part of herself with complete freedom. All that there is of love in me is a gift from Jesus, yet every gesture of love I am able to make will be recognized as uniquely mine. That's the paradox of grace. The fullest gift of grace brings with it the fullest gift of freedom. There is nothing good in me that does not come from God, through Christ, but all the good in me is uniquely my own. The deeper my intimacy with Jesus, the more complete is my freedom.

Whatever I am to be in the years ahead, anything that may be good about it comes from Jesus. But what comes from Jesus I can truly claim as most fully my own.

A little journey has come to its end. As I look up from my desk to the fog-covered trees of the forest of Compiègne, I realize that all I learned I knew already. But all I learned was also new. My only hope was to make Jesus more fully the center of my life, the heart of my heart, the lover of my soul, the bridegroom of my spirit. He was always there, in a soft, gentle, hidden way. Yet he is there now as though he had never been there. He is always the same and never the same, always absent, always present, always searched for, always found. That's what God's love is about. The Lover and the Beloved are two and yet one, separated and yet in full communion, in anguish yet filled with ecstatic joy. Mary and Bernadette knew about this. In Lourdes I caught a glimpse of it again. A new decade has begun; nothing can be predicted. Yet all is already held safe in the divine embrace that holds me, too.

About the Author

Henri J. M. Nouwen is a spiritual guide to many and author of thirty books. After he was ordained a priest in 1957 for the Archdiocese of Utrecht, Holland, he did graduate work in psychology at the Catholic University of Nijmegen and the Program for Religion and Psychiatry at the Menninger Clinic in Topeka, Kansas. In 1971 he received a degree in theology from the Catholic University of Nijmegen. He has taught courses in psychology, spirituality and pastoral theology at the University of Notre Dame, the Pastoral Institute in Amsterdam, Yale Divinity School and Harvard Divinity School. His living experiences have also been diverse: with the Trappists at Genesee Abbey, the poor in South America and the mentally disabled in France and Canada. Since 1986 he has been the pastor of the l'Arche-Daybreak community in Toronto, Canada.